Original title:
Lessons in Life from a Taco

Copyright © 2025 Creative Arts Management OÜ
All rights reserved.

Author: Victor Mercer
ISBN HARDBACK: 978-1-80566-041-5
ISBN PAPERBACK: 978-1-80566-336-2

Savoring Moments

In a world that rushes, take a pause,
A taco in hand deserves applause.
Each bite a treasure, delightfully messy,
With salsa drips that make you feel zesty.

Crunchy shell sings a joyful tune,
Fill it with joy, morning or noon.
Lettuce and cheese, a colorful play,
A feast that brightens up your day.

Refill Your Heart

When life gets tough, don't you fret,
Grab a taco, it's your best bet.
Stuff it with laughter, joy, and cheer,
With every topping, melt away fear.

A sprinkle of guac, a dollop of fun,
Sharing with friends, laughter weighs a ton.
Keep your heart full, let worries depart,
In the embrace of flavors, refill your heart.

The Spice of Life

Some days need a kick, a zesty bite,
Tacos are here, bringing delight.
Add jalapeños, feel the fire,
Life needs spice, it won't backfire.

From sweet to tangy, a flavor parade,
Every taco made, a masterpiece laid.
Seasoned with love, topped off with glee,
A culinary dance, wild and free.

Embracing Every Bite

Gentle crunch, a taco hug,
Savoring flavors, snug as a bug.
With every bite, a chance to rejoice,
Listen to your tummy, it has a voice.

So stuff them high, don't hold back,
In the world of tacos, you'll never lack.
Embrace the mess, don't fuss or fight,
Every taco moment feels just right.

Spice and Serenity

In a world full of flavors, oh what a blend,
A dash of spice makes boredom end.
Laughter and heat, they dance so bright,
A taco's charm brings pure delight.

With layers of joy, each bite a surprise,
Cheese melting gently, oh how it flies!
Wrapped in a shell, life's quirks to embrace,
Fun in each crunch, a savory grace.

Cumin's Call

Cumin whispers secrets of zest in the air,
Teasing the senses, a flavorful dare.
Life's not just mild when you spice it up,
Take a hearty bite, and wellness fills your cup.

Tortilla holds stories in every fold,
Adventures await, if only we're bold.
So roll with the punches, and savor the quest,
For in every taco, there's humor and jest.

Dances of Diced Tomatoes

Diced tomatoes jiggle, so fresh and bright,
Their tangy little steps bring sheer delight.
Chop, chop, chop—oh what a show,
In salsa's rhythm, let the good times flow.

Lettuce flies high like confetti in the sky,
Each crunch a reminder, don't wait, just try.
Life's a fiesta, so join in the fun,
With each little bite, you'll say, 'I've won!'

The Heart of a Taco

Under the surface, the goodness awaits,
A heart full of flavor, a plate that celebrates.
In laughter and fillings, we find our way,
Together we feast, come what may.

So gather your friends, don't let dreams stall,
Life's better shared, so let's have a ball.
With tacos, we toast to silliness and cheer,
In every bite shared, it all becomes clear.

The Heat of Challenges

In salsa's spice, we find our grit,
Each bite a trial, but oh, we commit!
Tortillas wrap what life throws our way,
With laughter and flavor, we seize the day.

When jalapeños set our tongues ablaze,
We learn to dance through the fiery maze.
Embrace the heat, don't run away,
For every challenge brings fun to play.

Juicy Discoveries

Tomatoes fine, we chop and slice,
In each fresh taste, we roll the dice.
The crunch of lettuce, a crisp surprise,
Unraveling secrets right before our eyes.

Avocado dreams, so silky and green,
They teach us soft is not often seen.
With every layer, there's more to find,
In taco pursuits, joy's intertwined.

A Recipe for Growth

A sprinkle of love, a dash of zest,
In every filling, we do our best.
Fold in the joys, the woes we face,
Mix it together, find your pace.

Sometimes we crumble, but that's okay,
A broken shell still finds its way.
In flavors blended, we come alive,
Growth in tacos will surely thrive.

Whispers of Tradition

Grandma's recipe, passed down the line,
With each bit shared, we feel divine.
The stories told wrapped up so tight,
In every taco, love takes flight.

From plates to hearts, the flavors flow,
Memories made as we gather and glow.
Celebrate what comes from the past,
In each juicy bite, we find the vast.

The Essence of Togetherness

A taco shared is joy declared,
Fill it up, don't be scared.
With salsa bright and cheese galore,
Friendship blooms with every score.

Gather 'round the table wide,
Pass the guac, let laughter slide.
We all have our layers to unfold,
In every bite, a story told.

Savory Surprises

Beneath the crunch, a treasure lies,
An unexpected flavor, oh what a prize!
With every nibble, a twist you chase,
Find joy in the pickle's embrace.

In life like tacos, don't hold back,
Try something spicy, not just a snack.
Embrace the surprises that spice our days,
For mundane moments can find new ways.

Simmering Expectations

Oh, don't assume the taco's fate,
Expect some heat, it's worth the wait.
Stir the pot, turn up the flame,
Life's a taco, never the same.

When served hot, things may spill,
Embrace the mess and feel the thrill.
With lettuce flying and sauce that drips,
Prepare for laughter from tasty trips.

Bite-Sized Wisdom

In small bites, we learn so much,
A sprinkle of this, a dash of that touch.
Chew through troubles, digest the fun,
Tacos unite us, one by one.

So next time life feels like a race,
Grab a taco, find your space.
Savor each layer, take it slow,
Wisdom's waiting in every flow.

The Savor of Simplicity

In a world of fancy dishes,
A taco shines so bright.
Wrapped in its humble glory,
It's simple and just right.

With just a bit of salsa,
And lime squeezed on the side.
What more do we need really?
Let flavors be our guide.

A stuffing of good fortune,
With beans and cheese combined.
Who needs a silver platter?
When happiness's aligned.

So here's to tasty moments,
In every tasty bite.
Savoring the small things,
Brings pure delight, alright!

Salsa Serenade

A dance of spicy flavors,
This salsa takes the stage.
Mixing heat and sweet together,
It sets the crowd to rage.

Just like in wild existence,
We need some zest and flair.
Too bland's a tightrope walker,
Let's swirl without a care.

With pico de gallo shimmy,
And guac that's smooth and green.
Life's better with some twirling,
And laughter in between.

So pour that salsa proudly,
In every taco round.
The rhythm of good eating,
Is joy that we have found!

Soft Shells and Hard Truths

A soft shell held together,
Hides truths we sometimes fear.
It's fluffy and forgiving,
But cracks when things get near.

When life seems all too fragile,
Embrace the tasty mess.
Each bite contains a lesson,
In flavors we confess.

A hard shell's got its secrets,
It won't bend or break.
Instead, it holds the filling,
For all of our own sake.

So take both kinds together,
And cherish every crunch.
For life's a mix of softness,
And truths to pack a punch!

The Art of Balance

In life's great taco making,
Balance reigns supreme.
Too much of one ingredient,
Will ruin all the dream.

A sprinkle of good humor,
With a dash of salty fun.
If life's a perfect taco,
Then laughter's number one.

Don't pack it all with pressure,
Let toppings find their space.
We need a touch of kindness,
To bring a smiling face.

So stack it up with care now,
And savor every bite.
For finding perfect balance,
Is truly pure delight!

The Comfort of Familiarity

A taco in hand, no fears to climb,
Wrap me tight, don't waste my time.
Layers stacked, just like my dreams,
Salsa drips, bursting at the seams.

Soft or hard, my taste buds cheer,
In every bite, the world feels near.
Familiar crunch, a smiling face,
In every taco, I find my place.

Spilling Secrets

When the taco talks, oh what a tale,
Of weekend feasts and chips that sail.
Lettuce whispers, cheese will grin,
Spices share where they've been.

Cilantro boasts of summer nights,
While onions cry, and so ignite.
Every crunch a secret spilled,
In taco talk, my heart is filled.

Culinary Connections

Tortillas wrap each funny fate,
Binding strangers on a plate.
Filling friendships, soft and warm,
A dip in guac, away from harm.

From side to side, the sauce does flow,
Each bite shared, the laughter grows.
In every taco, cultures blend,
Breaking bread, finding a friend.

From Corn to Culture

From maize to magic, a journey grand,
Each taco tells of distant lands.
Spicy tales and sweet delights,
In every fold, the world ignites.

Corn's soft cradle holds the spice,
Bringing joy like a roll of dice.
Wrapped in love, a tasty guise,
Open wide — surprise, surprise!

Drizzle of Clarity

In the bowl of guac, we find our truth,
A splash of lime brightens all our youth.
Chips may crumble, but we stand strong,
Dip into wisdom, where we belong.

Sour cream swirls like thoughts in our head,
A dollop of humor keeps worries dead.
With each bite, we savor the vibe,
Toppings together, feelings imbibe.

A Bite of Courage

With every layer built with intent,
A taco's heart never feels bent.
Take a leap with salsa so bold,
Life's best stories are often retold.

Lettuce wraps 'round like our dreams,
Crunching with laughter, bursting at seams.
Spicy surprises may come your way,
Courage is tasty, come what may!

The Crunch of Compromise

Soft shells whisper, hard shells call,
Finding middle ground in a tasty brawl.
Lettuce and beans, both take a seat,
Together they make life's flavors sweet.

Sauce tempers anger, a flavor divine,
In the taco world, all can align.
Crunching thoughts, they mesh and entwine,
In every bite, a lesson to dine.

The Dance of Ingredients

Tortilla spins, a cartwheel galore,
Dancing with veggies, they never bore.
Every ingredient joins in a whirl,
Together they flourish, giving life a twirl.

Tomato cha-cha with a hint of zest,
In this fiesta, we're all very blessed.
Join the salsa, let the flavors prance,
Life's a taco, so join the dance!

Tasting the Unexpected

In a taco shop, I took a seat,
With cheese and beans, my special treat.
But what's this flavor, oh so bold?
A dash of pickle? A tale unfold!

Each bite brings laughter from my mouth,
A fiesta humming, dancing south.
With random fillings, life's absurd,
Who knew a taco could speak a word?

The Tortilla of Time

Wrapped in tortillas, the moments lay,
Flour or corn, it's a buffet.
Some layers thick, some barely there,
Like memories fading, floating in air.

A bite of nostalgia, a crunch so clear,
The flavors of youth, taste buds cheer.
I savor the past, spice up the now,
In each little fold, I take a bow!

Spice Blends of Society

Cilantro whispers, "Join the fun!"
While jalapeños chase the sun.
In the pot of life, we mix and meld,
A dash of chaos, flavor compelled!

Corny jokes sprinkle, laughter's heat,
In this salsa dance, we all meet.
Pickled onions join the fray,
Building bonds in this tasty play.

The Palate of Perspective

A nacho chip once told a tale,
Of cheese so gooey, it'd never fail.
Like different views, each bite unique,
    A crunchy truth in every peak.

Guacamole's guile, smooth and sly,
It winks at the world, oh me, oh my!
With sour cream as a sweet disguise,
Life's complex flavors widen our eyes.

The Flavor of Resilience

When life gets messy, just hold it tight,
A squeeze of lime makes it feel just right.
Don't let the salsa spill on your shoe,
Embrace the chaos, it's part of the stew.

Tortillas can tear, but we patch them back,
With a dollop of cream, we'll stay on track.
Wrap up your troubles and take a big bite,
In the world of tacos, it's all black and white.

Dare to mix flavors, don't be afraid,
Every bite counts, let joy invade.
With each crunchy layer, we rise from the floor,
Life's a taco, so come back for more!

So when life gives you guac, spread it on thick,
Adding some spice, it'll do the trick.
Remember the lessons with each tasty crunch,
Laugh at the mess, and enjoy the munch!

Nibbles of Knowledge

In the kitchen of life, gather your friends,
Every salsa dip is where laughter transcends.
Chili peppers teach us to add some heat,
While shredded cheese makes each moment sweet.

Wrap your dreams tightly, don't let them fall,
A bit of jalapeño can spice up it all.
When onions make you cry, just let it flow,
Find joy in your tears, let the flavors grow.

Layers of goodness, don't rush through the stack,
Each tasty morsel is never a hack.
With every bite, there's wisdom to find,
Tacos prove true, "Life's better combined!"

So sprinkle some laughter, find joy in the meal,
Through onions and beans, let the funny reveal.
In this savory journey, let's all take a stand,
Knowledge is served in a taco so grand!

A Feast of Reflections

On a taco platter, life's flavors collide,
From black beans to corn, take them in stride.
A bite of perspective can clear your mind,
With a crunch of the shell, new truths you will find.

Sometimes it's messy, can't take it too slow,
Like spilled pico de gallo, just let it flow.
Each layer reveals a lesson or two,
Savor the insights, they're meant just for you.

So pass the hot sauce, don't fear the blaze,
Even a spicy moment can brighten the days.
With laughter and joy, let's feast in delight,
In this chaotic banquet, everything's right!

So pile on the toppings; don't shy away,
Embrace every flavor, come what may.
A taco's a canvas, a chance to reflect,
In the feast of our lives, let humor connect!

Cilantro Dreams

Rolling through life like a fresh tortilla,
Add a pinch of cilantro, spice up the idea.
Dance through the kitchen, let laughter ignite,
Who knew tacos could make everything bright?

With beans in a bowl and cheese in the pot,
Life's full of toppings that hit the right spot.
Don't fear the unusual, embrace each new taste,
In this taco adventure, there's never a waste.

So stack up your dreams like a taco supreme,
A sprinkle of humor is part of the theme.
Let's laugh at the mess and enjoy every bite,
In the world of tacos, everything feels right!

We toss in the guac and roll with the flow,
When served with a smile, let the good times grow.
Each bite tells a story, a flavorful shout,
In cilantro dreams, there's never a doubt!

Filling the Empty Spaces

Crunchy shell, oh what a sight!
Hiding treasures, both bold and bright.
Fill that gap with beans and cheese,
Life's too short to just appease.

Lettuce layers, fresh and green,
A sprinkle of spice, oh so keen!
Add a dollop of sour cream,
Every bite's a tasty dream.

Tomatoes diced with a zesty flair,
Bringing color to a meal laid bare.
Don't forget that salsa dip,
Life's a feast; take a big sip!

So when you're hungry, take a note,
Fill your plate, let laughter float.
In every scoop, find joy and play,
Enjoy the feast, come what may!

Nourishment in Diversity

Tortillas wrap so much within,
A world of flavors to dig in.
Meet spicy peppers, and guac so fine,
In every bite, let diversity shine.

Beans and meats, a dance in a bowl,
Each ingredient plays a role.
Mingle them well, don't be shy,
Celebrate life, let it fly high!

Chili heat and cilantro zest,
Different tastes, you know the best.
Together they sing in harmony,
Unity found in variety's spree.

So when you feast, don't just see,
There's magic in each recipe.
Embrace the mix, let flavors clash,
Life's a taco, take a splash!

The Art of Balance

In this taco, find your zen,
Soft and crunchy, the best blend.
Too much heat? Then ease it down,
For every frown, there's a crown.

Layer it well, don't spill the beans,
Life's like tacos — nothing means
A thing if unbalanced inside,
Wrap it up, let joy abide.

Sweet and savory, hold them tight,
Find your rhythm, keep it light.
Don't overload; let flavors play,
In perfect portions, hip-hip-hooray!

So savor each bite, nothing less,
Master the art, feel the finesse.
In every tortilla, learn the knack,
Balance your world, then smile back!

Flavors of Forgiveness

Mistakes happen, oh what a shock!
Like soggy lettuce or burnt corn rock.
But slather on some salsa bright,
Forgive the flaws, embrace the bite.

Grudges melt like queso warm,
In every taco, find your charm.
Share a bite, let laughter flow,
In messy moments, love can grow.

Spice it up and let it heal,
A sprinkle of joy is the deal.
Forget what's lost, let's savor this,
With every crunch, find laughter's bliss.

So take a bite, and taste the cheer,
With every flavor, draw near.
Forgive like tacos, be bold in zest,
Life's a feast; share it best!

Embracing Complexity

In a world wrapped tight, we often hide,
But each flavor inside gives joy a ride.
Sometimes we spill, and that's okay,
Messy moments brighten our day.

Salsa dances with rhythm and spice,
Every bite is a game, oh so nice.
Layers of goodness stacked high,
Embrace the chaos; let laughter fly.

Tortilla blank canvas, so vast,
Fill it up, make your moments last.
From beans to cheese, a tasty fest,
In our quirky mix, we find our best.

So take a bite, taste your delight,
In a taco's embrace, life feels right.
We're all a bit weird, and that's just fine,
So load it up, and let it shine!

Whispers of the Bean

In the quiet kitchen, beans softly chat,
"Life's all about balance! Just look at that!"
They share their tales, of joy and of strife,
Recognizing each twist is part of our life.

With a sprinkle of salt and a dash of glee,
They giggle about how tasty they can be.
In the dance of the spices, they find their groove,
Encouraging each other to always improve.

A dollop of sour cream adds smooth charm,
While chips on the side bring crunchy alarm.
"Let's mix things up! Don't you dare be bland!"
Say the beans as they wave their tasty hand.

So gather around, hear their sweet song,
In the taco ensemble where all belong.
With laughter and beans, every crunch can be,
A reminder of fun, life's great jamboree!

Life Served with Guacamole

Luscious green dip, oh what a delight,
Smooth like a hug, feels just so right.
With zest and a twist, it brightens the day,
A scoop of it brings smiles on the way.

Mixing in laughter, a squeeze of lime,
Every bite shared feels just sublime.
In life's messy bowl, don't worry or fret,
With guac by your side, you're never upset.

A chip takes a plunge, a gamble it makes,
In the bowl of joy, all worry forsakes.
Wonders of flavor, of chaos and fun,
Remind us to savor as we all run.

So grab your tortilla, embrace the green,
In this wild adventure, you can be seen.
With every delicious, creamy spread,
Life's tastiest moments will dance in your head!

The Boldness of Hot Sauce

A splash of the fiery, a daring delight,
Hot sauce struts in, ready to ignite.
"Take a chance!" it says with a wink,
Add a bit of spice, give your taste buds a link.

So sprinkle it on, feel the warmth rise,
Turning up the heat, watch the fun surprise!
With laughter erupting, and flavors galore,
We find that the bold can open the door.

In a world of bland, spice takes a stand,
With every hot drop, excitement is planned.
It teaches us all, not to hold back,
Life's a fiesta when you're on the right track!

So dab on that sauce, let the flavors collide,
In the taco parade, let's enjoy the ride.
Life's too short for a flavorless glaze,
Let's dive into spice and set hearts ablaze!

Wrapped in Encouragement

In a cozy shell, we find our place,
Filled with dreams, we join the race.
Toppings piled high, let's not be shy,
Together we rise, oh me, oh my!

Lettuce and beans, a crunchy duo,
With a dash of zest, we can steal the show.
Life may get messy, but don't you fret,
Just savor the ride, it's not over yet!

A pinch of humor, a sprinkle of fun,
Every bite we take, we've already won.
So wrap yourself tight, in joy and glee,
Embrace the flavors, just let it be!

Together we giggle, together we munch,
In this tasty life, let's all pack a punch.
So lift your taco, let spirits soar,
For in every wrap, there's room for more!

The Crunch of Reality

Life hits hard, like a good first bite,
Crunchy and bold, it feels just right.
Sometimes we crumble, sometimes we break,
But the fun part's finding what we can make!

A juicy mistake is just a surprise,
Like salsa that ends with a little spice.
We juggle our toppings, a colorful sight,
With each silly moment, our laughter ignites!

So embrace the crunch, let it be loud,
Dance with your tacos—hey, be proud!
Life's got tang, with all of its zest,
Chase down the flavors and simply invest!

Through the mess and the sauce, we come alive,
In this taco of life, we'll always thrive.
So grab a napkin, and don't you worry,
For in this wild feast, there's no need to hurry!

Salsa Secrets

A dollop of joy, a splash of delight,
Salsa's a secret that makes it all right.
Sometimes it's spicy, sometimes it's sweet,
Just like our journeys, it's quite a treat!

Life offers flavors, a smorgasbord wide,
We dip and we swirl, with arms open wide.
With a mix of the wacky, and swirls of the fun,
Every taco hour promises a home run!

In metered bites, we grasp our fate,
Salsa surprises can never be late.
So live in the moment, be bold in your quest,
Taste every salsa, and find what's best!

As spoonfuls collide, and giggles explode,
We roll through the laughter, lightening the load.
So savor the salsa; let flavors ignite,
For each moment we embrace is a true delight!

A Shell's Embrace

A shell so strong, holding dreams so tight,
Catered with kindness, it feels just right.
Life can be silly, but oh what a race,
In this taco journey, we find our place!

Beneath the surface, there's much to explore,
With every crunch, let's open the door.
The spice of our trials adds flavor to fate,
With laughter and friends, there's no room for hate!

In moments of madness, we gather around,
With tacos in hand, pure joy can be found.
So wrap it all up, with a wink and a grin,
In this colossal wrap, let's begin!

From guacamole dreams to cilantro surprise,
Life's a taco party, so don't compromise.
Let's raise our tortillas, toast to the fun,
For every good meal, is a race well run!

A Journey of Ingredients

In a tortilla, dreams wrap tight,
Beans and cheese, what a delight!
Spicy salsa joins the crew,
Together they blend, just like a stew.

Lettuce crunches, fresh and green,
Add some guac, it's fit for a queen!
Each bite a tale, flavors combine,
In this tasty world, we all dine.

Chili peppers, a fiery spark,
They bring the heat, igniting the dark.
Sour cream cools, a soothing balm,
In this fiesta, we all feel calm.

So take a bite, don't be shy,
Life's a taco, give it a try!
With every crunch, a story unfolds,
In a world of flavors, we're all told.

Unfolding in Warmth

Wrap me up in cheesy dreams,
Warm tortillas, bursting seams.
Sizzle of meat, oh what a sound,
In this fold, pure joy is found.

Tomatoes juicy, vibrant and red,
Instead of worries, let's be fed.
Onions add a kick, a playful bite,
Each layered story sparks delight.

Dip in the sauce, zest in the air,
Who knew meals could be this rare?
Every crunch, a reason to cheer,
With every bite, we shed a tear.

So let's dig in, and not feel meek,
In every taco, life's mystique.
Laugh and savor, let joy be your guide,
In this tasty world, let's take a ride.

The Dance of Toppings

Dancing salsa, hips that sway,
Jumping onions steal the day.
Crispy lettuce, twirls with grace,
In this taco, we find our place.

Guacamole mashes to the beat,
A velvety embrace, oh so sweet.
Cilantro flutters like a breeze,
With every topping, we aim to please.

Lime slices zing, a citrus jest,
A surprising burst, that's the best.
Layer it high, don't hold back,
In this fiesta, there's no lack.

So join the dance, don't be late,
A taco party, life's first-rate!
With laughter and joy, take your chance,
Together we make the perfect dance.

Seasoned Experience

Sprinkled wisdom, herbs so bright,
Seasoned tales in every bite.
Garlic whispers, spicy and bold,
In these flavors, stories told.

A dash of salt, a pinch of fun,
Mix it together, let's all run.
Cilantro dreams with hits of zest,
In this taco, we find our best.

Flip the tortilla, change your view,
Life's about trying something new.
Add a twist, make it yours,
In this creation, adventure soars.

So take a taste, savor the ride,
In every taco, there's joy inside.
With laughter to share and fun to glean,
In the flavor dance, we're all keen.

The Melodies of Flavor

A taco sings in spicy tones,
With laughter wrapped in crispy shells.
It knows just how to tickle bones,
And dance while all your taste bud swells.

Each bite a melody, a strike,
A harmony of zest and glee.
Like life, it's chaos on a hike,
But oh, the joy with each decree.

So grab your salsa, don't delay,
The guac awaits, a sidekick bold.
In every crunch, there's sweet ballet,
A banquet of the tales retold.

The taco knows it's all a game,
With every layer telling jokes.
It pokes at me, it plays the same,
Life's feast, where laughter gently pokes.

A Filling of Friendship

Gather 'round, my taco crew,
A filling shared with all my mates.
Our hearts unite, like beans and stew,
In every bite, our love translates.

We pile on toppings, never shy,
The cheese glues friendships like glue.
With laughter loud, we touch the sky,
Let's love like tacos, me and you!

Each droplet of salsa brings a cheer,
A story spun in tortilla wrap.
With every scoop, it's oh so clear,
We feast on joy, and take a nap!

So here's to every salsa spill,
To spicy nights and laughter's clout.
In every taco, friendship's thrill,
Filling hearts, there's never doubt!

Beans and Dreams

Beans are dreams in savory plots,
Steamy tales wrapped nice and tight.
With every spoon, life's tender thoughts,
Flavors swirl in jubilant flight.

I close my eyes with every bean,
To spicy places far and near.
They whisper secrets, loose and keen,
In every crunch, I feel the cheer.

From black to pinto, colors rise,
Each legume has its own sweet tale.
With a side of laughter, watch it fly,
Life's a taco, don't you bail!

For in each bite, a dream unfolds,
A chipper journey wrapped in fun.
So eat your beans, let laughter mold,
Together we shall dream, then run!

Coalescing Cultures

A taco's twist, a cultural blend,
From spices, stories, late-night chats.
Each layer wraps, as friendships mend,
In every bite, we share our hats.

From street taco to fancy feast,
Each corner holds a tale to tell.
In flavors new, let's share the least,
And celebrate in taco swell.

It's nachos here, and ceviche there,
With burritos joining in the fun.
Taco tales beyond compare,
In every plate, we all are one.

So let's unite in cheesy bliss,
As salsa dribbles, laughter flows.
Each taco kiss is pure, not miss,
In life's fiesta, everyone knows!

The Texture of Togetherness

In a wrap of warmth and flair,
We find love, without a care.
Each layer, packed with joys to share,
Together we feast, a tasty affair.

Crunchy edges, soft and sweet,
Bringing friends together to eat.
In every bite, laughter's the treat,
A recipe for joy, life's repeat.

From salsa dances to guac's embrace,
The journey of flavors, a joyful race.
In this mixture, we find our place,
For happiness thrives with every taste.

So, gather 'round, let's all unite,
In taco time, everything feels right.
With every munch, our spirits ignite,
The texture of love, a delicious sight.

Finding Comfort in a Tortilla

Wrapped up snug like a warm hug,
A tortilla's comfort, cozy and snug.
With a dash of spice, it gives a tug,
A moment of calm, life's little plug.

In a world that can feel so vast,
Finding warmth in a tortilla cast.
With every bite, worries are surpassed,
Together we savor, friendships amassed.

Like a good joke, it brings delight,
Even the beans put up a fight.
When life gets messy, it's always right,
To roll it up tight, and share a bite.

So let's toast to this savory shield,
In each tortilla, joys are revealed.
Finding comfort in this tasty field,
A simple wrap, our hearts are healed.

A Flavorful Perspective

Life's a taco, spicy and bright,
With a tangy twist and a hint of slight.
Each topping adds to the sheer delight,
But it's the sauce that makes it just right.

Take a bite, see the world anew,
Crispy or soft, what's your view?
Each flavor profile, a different hue,
With every crunch, there's something true.

Sometimes it's messy, but that's okay,
Embrace the spills, come what may.
For the quirks of life lead the way,
In the quirkiest bites, joy shall stay.

So pull up a chair, grab your plate,
Let's fill up our taco, it's not too late.
Life served spicy, let's celebrate,
A flavorful view, life's a great fate.

Spices of Change

Life is a taco, mixed with surprise,
Each spice a change, a new disguise.
From mild to wild, watch flavors rise,
In the kitchen of life, take the prize.

Cilantro whispers of fresh starts,
While jalapeños ignite kind hearts.
With every crunch, the adventure imparts,
The spice of change, where fun never departs.

So sprinkle joy, don't be afraid,
In life's big taco, some plans must fade.
The blend of stories in every shade,
With spice on our tongues, new dreams are laid.

Let's laugh as we blend, mix and twirl,
Embrace the chaos, give it a whirl.
For in every taco, life starts to unfurl,
A spicy journey, let's dance and whirl.

A Flavorful Journey

In a wrapper tight, dreams unfold,
Crunchy, soft, spicy, and bold.
Each bite a trip, no passport required,
Flavors dance, passion inspired.

Tomato, onion, a fiesta delight,
Making Mondays feel oh-so-bright.
With guac on the side, the party's complete,
Who knew tacos could offer such sweet treats?

The cheese melts slow, like time in the sun,
Every ingredient whispers, 'Join in the fun!'
Tortilla tales of friendships shared,
In every bite, love has been prepared.

So take a chance, don't be shy,
Life's too short; let flavor fly!
Wrap your worries in a warm embrace,
With a taco feast, forget the race.

Heritage in Every Layer

Layers of taste, with stories to tell,
Each crunchy shell casts a savory spell.
From grandma's kitchen, traditions unfold,
In each tasty bite, memories bold.

A dollop of history, a sprinkle of flair,
Tacos unite us, beyond compare.
From street carts bustling, to dinner tables,
Flavors connect us; they make us stable.

Cilantro sprinkles a cultural kiss,
Bringing together what we can't miss.
In every layer, joy we encounter,
A fiesta of flavors, our spirits they flounder.

So roll up your sleeves, and dig in deep,
These tasty treasures are ours to keep.
With every crunch, let laughter resound,
In taco love, our hearts are found.

Salsa of the Soul

A bowl of salsa, splashed with zest,
Stirring the heart, it's simply the best.
With each chip dunked in vibrant hues,
Even worries soften; joy comes in crews.

Heat and humor dance on my tongue,
Joyful chaos, like when we're young.
The spice of laughter mixed with our tears,
Dancing deliciously, calms all my fears.

A recipe of moments, chopped finely with care,
Together we stir, our burdens laid bare.
Where friendships bloom over flavors so bright,
Remember, my friend, we're always all right.

So come join this fiesta, let spirits unite,
With salsa of the soul, everything's right.
Let's sprinkle the fun, add laughter, not strife,
With each tasty bite, we savor this life.

Intersections of Taste

At the corner of crunch and creamy delight,
Tacos and tales make everything right.
Where flavors collide, oh what a scene,
A dance of textures, a culinary dream.

A pinch of this, a splash of that,
Creating a harmony: a taste diplomat.
Crossing cultures with joy on display,
Every taco party beckons, 'Come play!'

In the salsa rhythm, we sway and twirl,
Each bite igniting a flavor whirl.
On this canvas of taco, we paint with zest,
Finding connection, we're all truly blessed.

So gather your toppings, let's build our fate,
At the crossroads of flavors, we all celebrate.
With laughter and spice, let's savor the feast,
At the table of tacos, love never ceased.

The Journey of the Taco

In a world where flavors collide,
A taco rolls down with pride.
Through crunchy streets, it takes a ride,
With spicy dreams, it won't hide.

Beneath the sun, it finds some friends,
With salsa tight, the fun never ends.
Lettuce whispers, cheese transcends,
Together they dance, the joy it sends.

But beware the sour cream surprise,
It can cover up those eager eyes.
With each bold bite, adventure flies,
Life's a taco – oh, what a guise!

So roll with laughter, hold on tight,
In every taco, find your light.
A crispy shell or a soft delight,
Life's full of flavors – take a bite!

Layers of Love

Oh, the layers we build each day,
Like a taco stacked in a fancy display.
Guacamole dreams, we sprinkle and sway,
In this crunchy world, let's dance and play.

Life's not just meat; it's also the spice,
Happiness comes when you add a slice.
With every topping, be it cold or nice,
Embrace each layer – that's the best advice.

Sometimes you'll spill, but don't you fret,
Embrace the mess, it's not a regret.
Each drop of salsa, a joyful vignette,
In the taco of life, let's place our bet.

So gather your friends, share hearty laughs,
With every taco, feel the good halves.
Life's layers of love – no need for graphs,
In this funny feast, we find our paths!

Tacos and Truths

Crunchy truth wrapped in a shell,
Each bite tells stories we know so well.
The spicy chatter, the beans that swell,
In tacos, my friend, life's mysteries dwell.

Some like it hot, others like it mild,
In every bite, find the joy of a child.
Lettuce giggles, the queso's wild,
Tacos reveal truths, sweetly compiled.

Don't trust the toppings that promise too much,
Sour cream dreams can sometimes clutch.
Find your balance, savor the touch,
Tacos teach us... it's a hasty brunch!

Oh, how we feast on crunchy bends,
Finding the humor with every blend.
In righting the wrongs, let's not pretend,
For in this taco, the truth transcends!

Nourishment for the Soul

In the heart of a taco, warmth does reside,
Nourishment flows as flavors collide.
With each filled tortilla, worries subside,
In this funny dance, let's take a ride.

From nachos to quesadillas, oh what a feast,
In the salsa party, we're never least.
Sharing with friends, our joy released,
Every warm bite, our hearts are teased.

Wrap your dreams in a soft taco hug,
Life's simple joys, like a playful tug.
With every crunch, hear the laughter snug,
Nourishment comes from this delicious mug!

So gather 'round the table, no time to stall,
With each tasty taco, we've got it all.
For in every bite, both big and small,
We find nourishment, and we stand tall!

Cravings for Understanding

In the salsa dance, we find delight,
Spicy moments, both day and night.
Soft or crunchy, we make a call,
Every bite's a lesson, after all.

Wrapped in foil, a treasure we hold,
Surprises inside, both warm and bold.
Don't forget the toppings, piled so high,
Our choices reflect, like a taco pie.

With guacamole, we share our dreams,
A dollop of laughter, or so it seems.
Even tacos sometimes lose their way,
But with friends beside, we'll find our play.

So when life's messy, just give a crunch,
Add a sprinkle of cheese, enjoy your lunch.
For in every taco, there's wisdom found,
In bites of joy, together we're bound.

The Taste of Unity

Tacos unite, from near and far,
Each flavor a story, each bite a star.
From beans to cheese, we blend and mix,
In this feast of life, we find our fix.

Tomato red and lettuce green,
A taco's ensemble, a vibrant scene.
Layered together, we make a whole,
Sharing our flavors, feeding the soul.

Chalupas watch as friendships grow,
Each meal a memory, each crunch a glow.
We savor the moments, spicy and sweet,
For in unity, our lives are complete.

So gather round, with forks and cheers,
Embrace the taco, dismiss your fears.
For in every wrap, we taste the fun,
Celebrating together, we are as one.

Morsels of Mindfulness

Take a taco break, breathe in the zest,
Each bite a moment, life's little quest.
With jalapeños, we spice it right,
Mindful munching through day and night.

Lettuce whispers secrets, fresh and clean,
A crunchy reminder of all that's been.
Tomatoes plump, a juicy delight,
Savor each mouthful, make it bright.

In the sauce, there's a dash of grace,
Life's tangled issues, we slowly embrace.
Wrapped tight in a tortilla's hug,
A flavorful warmth, like a cozy rug.

So when you're lost, seek the taco's call,
Each morsel teaches, it's good for all.
With laughter and spice, we'll find our way,
Mindfulness served on a tasty tray.

A Sprinkle of Humor

Why did the taco cross the street?
To find the salsa and feel the heat!
With every crunch, a giggle unfolds,
Life's quirky flavor, so fun to hold.

Lettuce laughs while the beans joke around,
Each bite a punchline, joy abounds.
Tortilla wraps life's shenanigans tight,
A swirling fiesta, morning to night.

When life gets tough, just add some guac,
It's all about layers, like time on the clock.
Sardonic smiles in the face of mess,
Tacos remind us to laugh more, no less.

So sprinkle some humor on your plate,
In the taco of life, it's never too late.
For with every flavor, laugh in your soul,
Funny moments together make us whole.

Through the Tortilla

Beneath the tortilla, secrets lie,
Like salsa's splash and guacamole's sigh.
Wrap up your woes, let them slide,
With every bite, embrace the ride.

Frijoles spill stories, oh what a tale,
Of life's little messes and how they prevail.
Let cheese drizzle wisdom, so creamy and bright,
In the world of tacos, everything's light.

Don't fret the fillings, they all play a part,
Sometimes you're spicy, sometimes a sweet heart.
In every creation, you find your own groove,
As you savor the moments, get ready to move.

So dive in deep, don't let them forget,
Taco truths served on a platter, no debt.
With a crunch and a munch, life's lessons unfold,
In the embrace of tortillas, be bold.

A Crunching Awakening

Awake to the crunch of the morning's delight,
In the world of tacos, everything feels right.
Lettuce laughs gently, tomatoes all cheer,
As you ponder the truth lost in a smear.

A taco's a riddle wrapped tight in its shear,
A quesadilla whispering, 'Let go of your fear.'
Each layer a lesson, each taste a surprise,
With laughter and salsa, let joy arise.

Don't mind the spice, it's meant to ignite,
A feast of flavors, both day and night.
Gather round tables, share bites and your dreams,
In a world full of tacos, nothing's as it seems.

So munch on adventures, and crunch through the pain,
With every ingredient, wipe off the stain.
For life's little taco is yours to embrace,
Take a big bite, join the fiesta, and race!

Tacos as Teachers

Tacos stand ready, their wisdom in packs,
Teaching us laughter without any hacks.
With every soft tortilla we wrap up our fears,
A sprinkle of humor can dry all our tears.

Onions remind you to cry with delight,
While cilantro brings freshness, mood light as a kite.
Each flavor a lesson, in bite-sized fun,
In this delicious world, you're never outdone.

So embrace your fillings, let your heart flow,
With guac on the side, you're good to go.
In the circle of tacos, every moment's a dance,
With laughter and cheese, life offers romance.

So celebrate moments, crisp, warm, and bright,
In the feast of existence, every taco's a bite.
Tacos as teachers, they'll guide you along,
In the joyous rhythm, you'll dance to their song.

Wholesome Responsibility

A taco's a task, stacked high to the brim,
With each bite you take, make sure you don't skim.
Taking responsibility, that's how it's done,
Each topping a choice, a savory pun.

Sour cream moments, they bring on the smiles,
Navigating flavors, talking in styles.
The cheese lays its wisdom, so darn creamy and neat,
In the life of a taco, embrace every feat.

Crispy or soft, there's choice in each bite,
Tacos are a canvas, colorful and bright.
So juggle your guac, add some spice if you dare,
In the grand taco world, you're welcome to share.

So when life gets messy, just take a big crunch,
With lessons from tacos, it's always a munch.
Wholesome responsibility, so tasty and wise,
In every crunchy moment, let laughter arise.

Seasoned Journeys

In the market, spices dance,
Each flavor gets its chance.
Life's a mix of joy and strife,
Let's taco 'bout this crazy life.

Salsa drips with laughter bright,
Beans and rice make things alright.
Tortilla wraps the wildest dreams,
In every bite, a new theme.

Ingredients of Gratitude

Lettuce leaves remind to cheer,
Tomatoes bring camaraderie near.
Guacamole hugs like a friend,
Count your blessings till the end.

In every crunch, a spark ignites,
Taste of joy on taco nights.
Each layer tells a tale own,
Thankful hearts have brightly grown.

Toppings of Experience

Sour cream swirls like the past,
Every moment, hold it fast.
Chilies spice up the mundane,
Add a laugh to ease the pain.

Cheese melts like all our fears,
Stirring warmth through laughter and tears.
Each topping tells a story bold,
Of flavors new and memories old.

A Tasty Philosophy

Wrap it up, don't leave it bare,
Life's a taco, handle with care.
With extra zest and a hint of fun,
Take a bite, and you will run.

So savor each delicious layer,
Find your joy, that's the prayer.
In the mix of rich and sweet,
There's a crunch beneath your feet.

In the Name of Flavor

Toppings piled high, a sight to see,
Every bite brings discovery,
From beans to cheese, a tasty blend,
Even the sour cream we can befriend.

Salsa drips down, a zesty splash,
Unexpected mixes, but oh, how they clash!
Each flavor teaches, don't you know?
Embrace the chaos, let it flow.

In the crunch, there's joy to gain,
Sometimes it's messy, but never plain.
Sauce spills over, laughter will swell,
Every mishap is a story to tell.

So dive in deep, take a big bite,
Life's a feast, let's get it right!
With nachos too, don't you fret,
In flavor's name, we won't forget.

A Hard Shell of Strength

A crispy shell, it won't break,
Facing the heat, for goodness sake!
Inside it holds the tender heart,
You can't judge the shell from the start.

When filled with chaos, it stands tall,
Strength in layers, never to fall.
Tacos may bend, but they won't crack,
Resilience wrapped, let's keep on track.

When toppings tumble, don't dismay,
Just scoop them up, they're here to stay.
Like life itself, it's a snack parade,
Strength is found in the fun we've made.

So grab a taco, take a stance,
In the hard shell, we learn to dance.
With each delicious, crunchy bite,
We find our grit, oh what a delight!

The Spice of Resilience

A dash of spice can change the game,
In fiery salsa, never the same.
When life gets hot, just add some heat,
It's how we spice up our own beat.

Everything's bland without a spark,
A pinch of challenge keeps us smart.
Feeling bold? Toss in the pepper,
Life's best moments, we don't forget her!

From mild to wild, we can adjust,
With every sprinkle, it's a must.
A resilient bite tastes better still,
In every taco, we've got the will.

So taste the zest, don't shy away,
Let spice lead on, come what may.
The secret lies in daring to try,
With every flavor, we learn to fly!

Layers of Understanding

Stacked high with care, each layer placed,
Life's like a taco, in flavors we're graced.
From guac to beef, the blend's divine,
In every crunch, the truth we find.

With each layer peeled, a tale unfolds,
Stories of laughter, adventure retold.
Even with lettuce, crisp and bright,
Understanding grows, out of the light.

When veggies clash, don't be alarmed,
It's through the mix, we are charmed.
A slice of life, a dash of glee,
Every taco teaches, can't you see?

So savor each bite, take it slow,
With every layer, we learn and grow.
In this taco tale, we find delight,
In shared understanding, all feels right.

Filling the Layers of Existence

In a shell of crisp perfection,
We wrap our hopes and dreams.
Each layer tells a story,
Of laughter, love, and schemes.

Add some beans for heartiness,
And cheese for joy and flair.
A dash of hot salsa,
To spice up life and care.

Don't skip the guacamole,
It's creamy, smooth delight.
Just like life's little pleasures,
It makes everything feel right.

So pile it high and enjoy,
The messy, fun-filled chase.
For life is best experienced,
With a taco in its place.

Unraveling Spice in the Soul

What's life without a bit of zest?
A pinch of thrill and spice.
A taco's taste reminds us,
To savor every slice.

Lettuce on top like cool advice,
That crunches with a grin.
The colorful toppings emerge,
Like joys we find within.

Tomato drips like secrets,
Bold stories yet untold.
Sometimes sweet, sometimes tangy,
The flavors we behold.

With every bite a giggle,
A snack-sized revelation.
Flavors dance and twirl around,
A tasty celebration!

A Crunchy Epiphany

One bite was all it took,
For wisdom to unfold.
A taco held eternity,
In layers bright and bold.

A crunchy shell of laughter,
With stuffing close and tight.
Like friendships that surround us,
In every single bite.

Sour cream of misunderstandings,
But it only adds the fun.
Life's best when it's layered,
And shared with everyone.

So grab a seat, dive right in,
Let flavors take their toll.
In a world of tasty chaos,
Find the joy within your soul!

Wrapping Wisdom in Corn

In a tortilla's embrace,
Life's quirks all reside.
Folded snug in laughter,
Let your worries slide.

Corn holds all the secrets,
Of tricks both old and new.
Let's dance with fresh ingredients,
And share a laugh or two.

Like salsa that brings zing,
To a mundane platter,
Spice up your daily routine,
Make dull moments stagger.

So journey with your tacos,
In fun and tasty ways.
Wrap your heart in every bite,
And savor all your days!

A Journey Wrapped in Flavor

In the world of snacks, here's a tale,
A taco's voyage, never stale.
Wrapped in dreams, oh what a sight,
Toppings dancing, pure delight.

Lettuce crisp, and cheese that squeaks,
Mild and hot, the salsa speaks.
Life's a feast, with every bite,
Unexpected twists, such pure delight.

So gather 'round, take a leap,
Into flavors, where secrets keep.
With friends beside, there's joy in sharing,
A taco's life is worth declaring.

So savor each moment, don't just chew,
In every fold, there's something new.
Take a chance, don't let it pass,
In each great taco, find your sass!

Symphonies in Salsa

Twirling tomatoes, onion's grace,
Each chop's a note, a spicy embrace.
Cilantro sprigs like music's score,
Salsa's rhythm will make you roar.

Every taco, a serenade,
With flavors bold, and none afraid.
From crunchy shells to guac divine,
Life's a dance, and it's all mine.

Bite into laughter, chew on glee,
In every sauce, a melody.
So sing along with bites galore,
In our taco symphony, we all score!

Grab your friends, time to unwind,
In every scoop, new joys you'll find.
With every salsa, laugh and sway,
Life's a taco, let's dance today!

Tales of the Taco

Gather 'round for stories bold,
Of humble shells and treasures told.
In the land of spice, they weave and twine,
A tortilla magic, oh so divine.

Meet the taco, a beauty rare,
Dressed in beans, with flavor to spare.
Each bite's an adventure, full of cheer,
A fiesta waiting, year after year.

Guacamole dreams and pico zest,
In each taco, flavors are blessed.
Laughter spills like salsa on a plate,
In this crunchy world, we celebrate fate.

So here's to the filling, bold and bright,
In every taco, there's pure delight.
Let's munch away all worries and woe,
For tales of the taco make spirits glow!

Beyond the Shell

Beneath the shell, a world so vast,
With beans and cheese, a flavor blast.
Don't judge too quick, it wears a grin,
Each secret layer holds a win.

From crispy crunch to soft disguise,
Tacos tease with every surprise.
Variations dance, from mild to wild,
Life's a buffet; let's eat, my child!

So take a bite, and do not fret,
Adventure waits with every set.
Beyond the shell, there's much to find,
In this taco world, be unconfined.

Raise your hands, let laughter take flight,
In every taco, the world feels right.
Join the feast and let worries quell,
For happiness is found beyond the shell!

www.ingramcontent.com/pod-product-compliance
Lightning Source LLC
Chambersburg PA
CBHW051630160426
43209CB00004B/589